Salt

of the

Earth

Published in 2016 by Scene in Britain

A CIP record for this book is available from the British Library.

ISBN : 978 1 5272 0054 8

All photographs © Leonora Sheppard and © Roger Stayte

Design and Production : Roger Stayte

Recipes : as individually credited

CONTENTS

INTRODUCTION

This is not a cookbook, it's more than that.

As you open this book you may be thinking, "Oh no, not another cookbook". In an era when we're overwhelmed with media on food, what to eat and how to eat it, this is not another lifestyle guide or nutritional magic bullet to add to your shelves. This is a collection of recipes donated by residents of Affpuddle, Briantspuddle and Turnerspuddle, to help create a book which gives a glimpse of our parish today, as well as being a method of fundraising.

Mary Nesling suggested the idea of bringing together a collection of recipes from the parish as an alternative fundraising idea. The concept was to gather recipes that have been handed down through the family, passed from neighbour to neighbour or just a household favourite. Here is that collection and we have illustrated it with images from the parish, photographed through the seasons to give a snapshot of rural life, what we're eating, what we're growing, the animals we're keeping and the landscape we're surrounded by. It's interesting to see the variety of recipes, from British classics to those with international influences, that are all part of our daily fare.

The proceeds from the sale of this book will go to Briantspuddle Village Hall. The village hall was originally built with cob walls, oak beams and a thatched roof. A charming element of the village, but this lovely building creates the same challenge that faces many communities up and down the land - fundraising.

The added cost of maintaining an historic building and working with traditional materials creates a continual drain on parish coffers. All villages have an army of volunteers keeping their village afloat on cups of tea and rafts of cake with parishioners unwaveringly loyal in their support of cream teas, open gardens, fayres, fetes and fun-days. This is simply another string to that bow, that will hopefully sit on your bookshelf or coffee table to be enjoyed and referred to for years to come.

Whilst thumbing through its pages you can feel a warm glow of pride knowing your purchase has helped keep a small community and a little part of the nation's heritage together.

All of the recipes, food, props, photography, design and associated time in producing this book have been entirely donated. All the images have been photographed over the last twelve months, with the exception of the snow scenes which were shot in 2010.

Thank you for buying this book.

Leonora Sheppard & Roger Stayte
Dorset, 2016

Briantspuddle Village Hall
Dorset
2014

ACKNOWLEDGEMENTS

Many thanks go to Mary Nesling for suggesting the idea of this book.

A massive round of applause to all the residents of the parish who took the time to contribute recipes — without them there simply wouldn't be a book.

Grateful thanks to the following people for their generous support and assistance in bringing this project to life;

Audrey Grindrod

Elizabeth and Frank Guinn

Karen Harper

Peter Head

Sarah Lowman and Ian Kaye

Tricia and Ken Kilbank

Julia and Ken Olisa

Carole and Trevor Poole

Shirley and Roger Prideaux

Mike Rabjohns

Christine and Derek Ralls

Pauline and Phil Samways

and all our local landowners

NOTES ON THE RECIPES

The recipes, ingredients and methods are as supplied by the donator of the recipe.

Although all reasonable care has been taken in the preparation of this book, neither the publisher nor the author can accept liability for any consequence arising from the use thereof, or from the information contained therein.

All cooking times are approximate and will vary from conventional oven to fan-assisted oven or Aga.

All teaspoon **(tsp)** and tablespoon **(tbs)** measurements are based on measuring spoons where:

$$1 \text{ teaspoon (tsp)} = 5 \text{ ml}$$
$$1 \text{ tablespoon (tbs)} = 15 \text{ ml}$$

A '+' symbol within the ingredients list indicates no specified amount, the ingredient or spice can be added to personal preference.

For convenience, we have listed all ingredients and temperatures in both metric and imperial systems.

All conversions from imperial to metric and vice versa are approximate.

Happy hour

Lemonade

INGREDIENTS	imperial	metric
Lemons	2	2
Water, boiling	1 pint	570 ml
Sugar	4 oz	110 g

Wash the lemons and grate the rinds.

Place the rind and sugar in a jug.

Pour the boiling water over them.

Cover the jug and let it stand until cool.

Add the juice of the lemons.

Strain the lemonade and use.

Dilute with water, lemonade or soda water.

Fiona Hogger
Briantspuddle

Trevor's Cider

INGREDIENTS	imperial	metric
Apples		
Sugar		
Water		

Gather your apples.

Open a flagon of last years' cider and invite round all your friends for an afternoon of apple peeling and putting the world to rights.

Press your apples

Collect the juice

Ferment

Add sugar and love

Store

Enjoy

Trevor Poole
Briantspuddle

Sex on the Beach

INGREDIENTS	imperial	metric
Vodka	1 fl oz	30 ml
Peach schnapps	1 fl oz	30 ml
Orange juice	1½ fl oz	45 ml
Cranberry juice	1 fl oz	30 ml
Lemon, a squeeze of juice	+	+

Pour all the ingredients into a cocktail shaker, give it a good shake and serve with ice.

A group of eight of us in Affpuddle and Briantspuddle, all ladies, get together around the time of our birthdays, and the birthday girl cooks lunch for the other seven.

Each of us has some little speciality that is a regular feature of her own party, and this cocktail is something I usually serve as an aperitif. Its racy title causes a lot of mirth, particularly as the total age of the eight of us does not fall that much short of 700!

The quantities I give are as for the original recipe for this cocktail, but for our parties I reduce the alcohol content to less than half and increase the fruit juices to a quantity for a tall glass as everyone has to get home safely!

Diana Holman
Affpuddle

Elderflower Champagne

INGREDIENTS	imperial	metric
Elderflower heads	7	7
Lemons	2	2
Water, boiled	1 gallon	4.5 litres
Sugar	1¼ lb	570 g
Cider vinegar	2 tbs	30 ml

You'll need: A large bucket or fermentation bucket if you have one.
Muslin or a fine sieve.
Bottles – sparkling wine bottles with wired corks or screw topped bottles. Re-used bottles should be clean and sterilised.

Place the sugar in the bucket and pour over the boiled water. Stir until all the sugar is dissolved and leave to go cold.

Add the elderflowers, lemons and cider vinegar and leave it all to soak for 24 hours.
Strain the liquid through a muslin or very fine sieve.

Pour into the clean bottles. Don't screw on the tops very tightly as the drink will want to work itself out of the bottle for another week or so.

It will only keep for about 3 months, but you'll have drunk it in a sunny corner of the garden by then...

My mother, Olive, used to make a lot of homemade wine particularly in the '70's and I remember fermentation buckets lining the kitchen and flagons gurgling in the airing cupboard. Parsnip wine, pea pod wine, dandelion, broad bean, ginger, blackberry and more...quite a hair curling assortment.

I was too young to imbibe but it seemed to have the desired effect on friends who were brave enough to share in the wine. These days I think you could run your car off it, but one brew that I did help with and enjoy on the lazy days of summer was Elderflower Champagne.

Leonora Sheppard
Briantspuddle

Sloe Gin

INGREDIENTS	imperial	metric
Sloes	1½ lb	750 g
Sugar	4 oz	110 g
Gin	2 pints	1.2 litres

First gather your sloes, and if you like to uphold country folklore, this should be after the first frost.

Pour yourself a glass of last years' sloe gin and settle down at the kitchen table to prick the sloes with a darning needle.

Place the sloes in a large screw-top or kilner-style jar and cover with the sugar. Leave to steep in a dark place for 3-4 days, then add the gin and store for 3-4 months back in the dark.

Give the jars an occasional shake.

Strain the liquid into bottles and store for at least 12 months.

It's worth the wait.

Duncan Sheppard introduced me to the delights of sloe gin one winters' evening in front of the fire. It's countryside chemistry in a bottle.

Roger Stayte
Briantspuddle

Let's get started

Butternut Squash & Bacon Soup

INGREDIENTS	imperial	metric
Butter	1 oz	30 g
Butternut squash, peeled, seeds removed, chopped into small potato size pieces	1 lb	500 g
Onion, large, chopped	1	1
Garlic clove, crushed or chopped	1	1
Stock, chicken or vegetable	18 fl oz	500 ml
Single cream, optional	4 fl oz	100 ml
Bacon rashers	3	3
Nutmeg	½	½
Salt & Pepper	+	+

Melt butter in a large enough heavy bottomed pan.

Add bacon, garlic and onion for a few minutes and then add the squash. Cook for 10-15 minutes stirring frequently.

Grate in the nutmeg, pepper and salt and cook for a further 5 minutes.

Add the stock, bring to the boil and simmer on a lower heat until tender (if you have an Aga, put in bottom or simmering oven for an hour or two).

Blend all the ingredients until smooth and then stir in the cream if using it.

Season to taste and serve with crusty bread.

Always tastes good and even I can make it!

Phil Scrase
Briantspuddle

34

Nettle Soup

INGREDIENTS	imperial	metric
Olive oil	1 tbs	15 ml
Butter	2 oz	60 g
Onion, large	1	1
Leek, small	1	1
Garlic cloves, whole	2	2
Nettle tops	1 lb	460 g
Stock, chicken or vegetable	2 pints	1.1 litre
Double cream	2 fl oz	60 ml
Salt & Pepper	+	+

You'll need a pair of thick gardening gloves...

First collect your nettles. Ideally use young nettle tops only, but leaves and tops of older nettles still work. Wash well to remove any unwanted dust and snails.

Finely chop the onion and leek. Heat the butter and oil together and sweat the chopped vegetables with seasoning until soft. Add the nettles and the whole garlic cloves. (The garlic should add a gentle infusion rather than over power), and sweat for 5 minutes. Add the hot stock and bring up to the boil. Simmer for 5–10 minutes depending on the age of your nettles. If preferred, remove the garlic cloves at this stage.

Liquidise the soup and return to the pan on a low heat. Stir in the cream and adjust seasoning to taste.

Packed with vitamin C and a great way to recycle garden weeds.

Leonora Sheppard
Briantspuddle

Watercress and Potato Soup

INGREDIENTS	imperial	metric
Onion, small	1	1
Watercress, bunches that are washed and roughly chopped	2 bunches	2 bunches
Potatoes, peeled and chopped	8 oz	230 g
Stock, vegetable	14 fl oz	400 ml

Heat some vegetable oil in a large saucepan.
Add the vegetables. Cover and cook gently for 5 minutes.

Add the stock, bring to the boil then lower the heat and
simmer for 30 minutes stirring occasionally.

Allow to cool a little before blitzing with a hand blender
or in a liquidiser.

Adjust seasoning as necessary. Serve hot.

Nicky and Richard Killer
Briantspuddle

Lentil Pâté

INGREDIENTS	imperial	metric
Split Red lentils	½ lb	230 g
Garlic clove, large	1	1
Lemon, juice only	½	½
Tomato purée	1 tbs	15 ml
Parsley, chopped	1 tbs	15 ml

Cook the lentils in salted water for 15-20 minutes.
It is important that you drain the lentils very well.

Chop the garlic.

Put all the ingredients into a blender and blend
until smooth.

Serve with hot whole wheat bread or pitta bread.

*Another favourite from the 'Down to Earth
Cookbook' that's so flavoursome and easy to make.*

Mary Nesling
Briantspuddle

Smoked Mackerel and Apple Cocktail

INGREDIENTS	imperial	metric
Smoked mackerel	8 oz	230 g
Oil and vinegar dressing	¼ pint	140 ml
Sour cream	¼ pint	140 ml
Orange rind, finely grated	1	1
French mustard	1 tsp	5 ml
Apples, Cox's Orange Pippin	3	3
Salt & Pepper	+	+

Flake the smoked mackerel into a bowl and mix in the other ingredients, chopping the apples fairly small.

Mix all together then put into prawn cocktail type glasses and garnish with watercress.

Serve with triangles of thinly cut brown bread.

The following recipes are the favourites taken from the menus of a pub in Berkshire (in the Egon Ronay 'Good Food Guide' of hundreds of years ago...... well, over fifty) when I worked there.

Miss Waterhouse used to stay at the pub. I was very embarrassed when we first came to the village and she invited us to tea and on recognising me I reminded her that she had tipped me half a crown 'for stockings dear' when I carried her suitcase upstairs!

Sue Taylor
Briantspuddle

Salmon Mousse

INGREDIENTS	imperial	metric
Salmon, tinned	8 oz	230 g
Butter	4 oz	110 g
Potatoes, small, cooked	5	5
Vegetable oil	1 tbs	15 ml
White wine vinegar	1 tbs	15 ml
Cochineal, optional - a tiny splash for additional colouring	+	+
Salt & Pepper	+	+

Blend together the salmon with the cooked potatoes until smooth. Add the remaining ingredients and mix well until thoroughly combined.

Line a **1lb ¦ 450g** loaf tin with cling-film and fill with the mixture. Place in the fridge and chill for at least 12 hours.

Arrange lettuce leaves on a plate and turn out the salmon mousse on top of the leaves. Decorate the edges with slices of cucumber. Cut into slices and serve as a first course.

This can also be made using cooked ham instead of salmon.

This is a popular course with the ladies who lunch in Briantspuddle.

Sheila Kayll
Briantspuddle

Hangop

INGREDIENTS	imperial	metric
Plain yoghurt, a large pot	1	1
Salt and freshly ground pepper, to taste	+	+
Flavourings or your choice...	+	+

Place a clean dish towel or muslin cloth in a strainer over a bowl.

Pour in the yogurt and tie up the cloth with string. Hang it over a bowl/bucket/sink overnight or for longer if you prefer. The idea is to let all the whey drain out of the yoghurt. You can give the cloth a squeeze from time to time to get rid of excess moisture.

When it is time, scrape the remaining yoghurt into a bowl. The result is a soft cheese to which you can add a variety of flavourings.

Choose from:
Salt, pepper, fresh chopped herbs (chives work well), crushed garlic, olive oil, finely chopped dried tomatoes, harissa, chopped jalapeno peppers, pesto etc!

Serve with rye bread, biscuits or toast.

Here is a savoury alternative to Oma's White pudding (p.168) called Hangop, which means 'hang up' in Dutch, for obvious reasons.

Kate Gainsford
Briantspuddle

Cheese Soufflé

INGREDIENTS	imperial	metric
Butter	1½ oz	45 g
Flour	1 oz	30 g
Milk	½ pint	290 ml
Cheese, grated	3 oz	90 g
Eggs, yolks	4	4
Eggs, whites	4	4
Salt & Pepper	+	+

Preheat oven to hot **425°F ¦ 220°C ¦ Gas 7**

Make a white sauce with the butter, flour and milk.

Add grated cheese, stirring all the time. Season with salt and cayenne pepper, remove from the heat and beat in egg yolks one at a time. Leave in a warm place while you whisk egg whites to a firm snow.

Add one tablespoon of egg whites to the sauce, stir it in, then fold in remaining egg whites, add more salt and cayenne if necessary, then turn lightly into a soufflé dish (large enough to allow the soufflé to rise).

Put into a pre-heated oven, turn heat down to **400°F ¦ 200°C ¦ Gas 6** and bake for 20 to 25 minutes.

Serve straight away when top is browned, puffy, and soufflé is even a bit sloppy.

Eat at once.

Serves 4 small helpings

Frances and John Solly
Affpuddle

Mint Jelly

INGREDIENTS	imperial	metric
Cooking apples	2 lb	920 g
Vinegar	1 pint	570 ml
Sugar	1 lb	460 g
Mint leaves, chopped	3 tbs	45 g

Wash some cooking apples. Core and weigh them.

To every 2lb of fruit add 1 pint of vinegar.

Boil until soft.

Strain.

To every pint of liquid add 1lb of sugar.

Boil.

As it sets, beat in 2–3 tablespoons of chopped mint.

Pour into jars and cover.

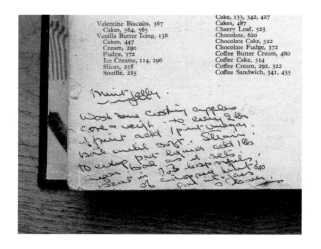

My grandmother had written this on the corner of the back page of her 1958 copy of Good Housekeeping Cookery Compendium.

Heather Griffith
Briantspuddle

Spiced Oranges

INGREDIENTS	imperial	metric
Oranges	10	10
White wine vinegar	1 pint	570 ml
Sugar, soft brown or granulated	2½ lb	1.13 kg
Cinnamon stick	1	1
Cloves	30	30

Sterilise several screw top or Kilner-style jars. Wide necked jars are best to fit in the orange slices.

Slice the oranges without peeling them, about ¼" ¦ **5mm** thick.
Lay the slices in a large pan and cover with water. Simmer with lid on until the peel is tender, approximately 20 minutes. Drain the oranges reserving the cooking liquid.

In another pan place the vinegar, sugar and spices. Boil together for a few minutes.

Carefully add the orange slices to the vinegar and spice liquid and add a couple of spoonfuls of the cooking liquid. Simmer gently for 30-40 minutes until the oranges turn clear. Using a slotted spoon, carefully layer the orange slices into your clean jars. Pour off any excess syrup back into the pan.

Bring the syrup to a boil and boil hard to reduce by about half. Pour the syrup over the sliced oranges in their jars until covered. Allow to cool and then seal.

Store in a cool dark place for at least two weeks.

Delicious with cold meats, especially gammon and turkey.

This recipe came from Faith Russel who lived at No. 2 Briantspuddle and it became a firm favourite of my mother Olive, and it graced every Christmas table.

Leonora Sheppard
Briantspuddle

Time to eat

Puy Lentil, Red Onion and Sun-dried Tomato Salad

INGREDIENTS	imperial	metric
Puy lentils, picked over to remove stones	8 oz	230 g
Bay leaf	1	1
Red wine vinegar	1 tsp	5 ml
Garlic cloves, peeled and left whole	2	2
Caster sugar, just a pinch	+	+
Salt & Pepper	+	+
Onion, large	1	1
Sun-dried tomatoes in oil, drained and chopped	1¾ oz	50 g
Balsamic vinegar	2 tbs	60 ml
Olive oil, extra virgin	4 tbs	60 ml
Goat's cheese or Feta cheese, crumbled	4 oz	110 g
Flat leaf parsley, chopped	3 tbs	45 ml

Put the lentils in a pan with the bay leaf, vinegar, one whole garlic clove, sugar and seasoning. Cover with **2 pints ¦ 1.2 litres** cold water, bring to the boil and leave to simmer for about 25 minutes, until the lentils are just tender but still holding their shape. Drain the lentils, discard bay leaf and whole garlic clove.

Place in a salad bowl and leave to go cold. Finely chop the remaining garlic clove and stir into the lentils with the rest of the ingredients. Season to taste and chill for two hours to let the flavours soak into the lentils before serving.

Doreen and Steve Sanderson
Affpuddle

64

Jellied Beetroot Mould

INGREDIENTS	imperial	metric
Beetroot	3½ lb	1.6 kg
Water	6 fl oz	170 ml
Tarragon or White wine vinegar	6 fl oz	170 ml
Caster sugar	3 tbs	45 ml
Gelatine	¼ oz	15 g
Salt & Pepper	+	+

You will need a **2½ pint ¦ 1.5 litre** mould or bowl.

Scrub the beetroot and leave whole with the roots and tops on. If you cut them off they'll bleed during the cooking process.

Place the beetroot in a large pan and cover with cold water, add ½ **tbs ¦ 10g s**alt and bring to the boil. Simmer until tender - approximately an hour. This will depend on the age and size of the beetroot. Leave to cool in the cooking liquid and then rub off the skins.

Place the vinegar, water and sugar into a pan and sprinkle the gelatine over the top. Leave for a few minutes to allow the gelatine to swell and then dissolve over a gentle heat. Season with salt and pepper.

Slice the beetroot and arrange the slices in a clean dry bowl or mould in neat layers. Pour the liquid over the top until it comes to the top of the bowl. Leave overnight to set.

Sprinkle the plate you intend to serve the mould on with a little cold water. Dip the bowl into a basin of hand hot water which should loosen the mould. Place the serving plate on top, and holding firmly reverse the plate and mould over and slide off the bowl.

If your mould is not central on the serving plate the sprinklings of water should enable you to reposition the mould on the plate.

Decorate the mould with sliced hard boiled eggs and sprigs of watercress.

Carole Poole
Briantspuddle

Couscous with Grapes and Cucumber

INGREDIENTS	imperial	metric
COUSCOUS		
Couscous	12 oz	340 g
Boiling water or vegetable stock	14 fl oz	400 ml
Olive oil	3 tbs	45 ml
Onion	1	1
Ground cumin	2 tsp	10 ml
Ground coriander	2 tsp	10 ml
Mixed spice	2 tsp	10 ml
Cardamom pods, seeds removed and ground	1 tsp	5 ml
Garlic cloves, crushed	2	2
Chick peas, (tinned), drained	14 oz	400 g
Whole almonds	2½ oz	75 g
Chilli sauce, medium	2 fl oz	60 ml
Mint and parsley sprigs, chopped	2	2
Lemon, juice	1	1
Salt & Pepper	+	+
GRAPES & CUCUMBER		
Butter	½ oz	15 g
Cucumber, peeled and chopped into large chunks	14 oz	400 g
Red grapes, seedless	7 oz	200 g
Salad onions, chopped	3 oz	90 g
Lemon, juice	1	1

Couscous

Mix the couscous in a bowl with the boiling water/vegetable stock. Cover and set aside for 10 minutes.

Cook the onion in the olive oil until soft.

Mix the ground spices together. Add to the onion with the garlic. Stir over a medium heat for 2 minutes.

Add the chick peas, almonds and chilli sauce. Stir over a medium heat until sizzling.

Fluff up the couscous with a fork. Add to the spicy mixture.

Just before serving, heat briefly and add the mint, parsley and lemon juice. Season.

Cucumber and grapes

Melt the butter in a frying pan. Add the cucumber and grapes. Sauté until the grape skins start to blister.

Stir in the lemon juice and salad onions.

Serve the couscous onto plates. Top with the sizzled cucumber and grapes. Garnish with fresh mint.

Julia Olisa
Briantspuddle

Cranberry and Green Lentil Salad

INGREDIENTS	imperial	metric
Dried Cranberries	5½ oz	150 g
Green Lentils, (14oz ¦ 410g tins) drained and rinsed	3 tins	3 tins
Parsley, a large bunch, chopped	1 bunch	1 bunch
Olive oil	4 tbs	60 ml
White wine vinegar	1 tbs	15 ml
Oranges, zest and juice	2	2

Soak the cranberries in the orange juice until they're plump.

Mix together the orange zest, lentils and parsley.

Add to cranberries and orange juice and mix well.

Whisk the olive oil and vinegar together and pour over.

Season lightly.

Diana Holman
Affpuddle

BBQ'd Head of Garlic

INGREDIENTS	imperial	metric
whole garlic bulbs - as many as you like...		

On a barbeque, set up your grill for indirect heat by placing the coals towards the outside edges.

If the stalk is still left on the garlic, cut it off.

Place each head of garlic on a piece of foil, sprinkle with a little salt if desired and wrap the foil around the head with a twist at the top.

Place on the barbeque and turn the foil wraps every now and again.

Roast for about 30 minutes or until it's soft - a gentle squeeze with fingers or tongs is the best way to tell.

Mike Rabjohns
Briantspuddle

Coronation Chicken at the Forty's

INGREDIENTS	imperial	metric
Chicken breasts	20 pieces	20 pieces
Mild curry powder	2 tbs	30 ml
Mayonnaise	1 pint	570 ml
Apricot purée	2 tbs	30 ml
Double cream	1 pint	570 ml

Serves 20 people.

Poach the chicken breast in chicken stock.
Allow to cool and cut into bite sized pieces.

In a large bowl mix together all the other
ingredients.

Add more curry powder or apricot to taste.

Season with black pepper and salt and fold in the
cooked chicken pieces.

Anne Forty
Briantspuddle

Courgette Fritters

INGREDIENTS	imperial	metric
Courgettes	½ lb	230 g
Egg, large	1	1
Plain flour, plus a bit extra for coating	2 tbs	30 ml
Feta cheese, broken into chunks	½ packet	½ packet
Mint and parsley, a handful, chopped	+	+

Grate the courgettes into a clean tea towel and then squeeze out the excess moisture. Tip into a bowl and mix in all the other ingredients.

Place 1 heaped tablespoon of the mixture in some flour and coat on all sides, repeat process making six fritters in all.

Heat some oil in a frying pan then place the fritters in the pan and fry until golden.

Doreen and Steve Sanderson
Affpuddle

Scoblianka

INGREDIENTS	imperial	metric
Veal	1 lb	460 g
Mushroom, button or sliced	5 oz	140 g
Onion, sliced	5 oz	140 g
Calvados	3 fl oz	90 ml
Vermouth, a dash	+	+
Cream	½ pint	290 ml
Salt & Pepper	+	+
Sage	+	+

Cut the veal into strips and fry in butter until brown.

Add the mushrooms and onions and sweat them until the onions are cooked.

Add the Calvados and a dash of Vermouth.

Put in the oven for about fifteen minutes then bring out and onto a hot ring and add cream and boil until it thickens.

Add salt, ground black pepper and sage to taste.

Serve with rice.

Another favourite recipe taken from the menus of the pub in Berkshire (in the Egon Ronay 'Good Food Guide' of hundreds of years ago......well, over fifty) when I worked there.

We used to sell this for 14 shillings and six pence!

Sue Taylor
Briantspuddle

Savoury Herby Bread & Butter Pudding

INGREDIENTS	imperial	metric
Eggs	6	6
Single cream	½ pint	290 ml
Mustard	1 tbs	15 ml
Slices of bread, stale, white	7	7
Chives, chopped	1 tbs	15 ml
Thyme, chopped	1 tbs	15 ml
Parsley, chopped	1 tbs	15 ml
Cheddar cheese, grated	4 oz	110 g
Salt & Pepper	+	+
Nutmeg	+	+

Grease an ovenproof dish.

Beat the eggs, cream and mustard together and season with salt, pepper and nutmeg to taste. Cut the bread into squares (approx. **1"** ¦ **2cm**) and put half the squares into the ovenproof dish. Sprinkle the herbs and half the cheese over the bread. Cover with the remaining bread and cheese. Pour the egg and cream mixture over and leave standing for at least 6 hours or overnight.

Bake in the oven for about 20 minutes or until the surface is nicely browned and all the liquid has been absorbed.

Serve with salad for a vegetarian supper or as a side dish instead of potatoes.

Karin Gray
Briantspuddle

Singapore Pork

INGREDIENTS	imperial	metric
MEAT		
Lean pork	1 lb	460 g
Soy sauce	2 tbs	30 ml
Green pepper, de-seeded and chopped	1	1
Pineapple pieces, tinned	8 oz	230 g
Tomatoes, skinned and chopped	6	6
Plain flour	+	+
SAUCE		
Water, boiling	¾ pint	430 ml
Cornflour	2 tbs	30 ml
Ketchup	4 tbs	60 ml
Soy sauce	4 tbs	60 ml
White wine vinegar	4 tbs	60 ml
Sugar	4 tbs	60 ml

Cut the pork into bite size pieces. Mix with soy sauce and marinade for several hours.
Lightly flour the pork and fry in oil until crisp. Drain on kitchen paper.
Mix together the chopped pepper, pineapple and tomatoes and lightly fry until softened. Mix together with the pork and place in an ovenproof dish.

Mix the cornflour with a little cold water and then add to the boiling water. Add the sugar, ketchup, soy sauce and vinegar. Mix and pour over the meat and fruit mixture. Season with black pepper and salt.

Cook in a medium oven until the meat is tender.

Chips Badcock
Briantspuddle

Garlic, Lemon and Parsley Roasted Pheasant Breast

INGREDIENTS	imperial	metric
Pheasant breasts	4	4
Butter, salted	4½ oz	125 g
Lemon, juice and zest	1	1
Parsley, a handful, chopped	+	+
Garlic cloves	4	4

Soften the butter and add the lemon, parsley and crushed garlic cloves. Mix really well and slather the pheasant breasts with the mixture.

Put the pheasant breasts in a roasting tray and roast at **450°F** ¦ **230°C** ¦ **Gas 8** for 20 minutes.

Leave the pheasant breasts to rest for 10 minutes, spooning some of the melted flavoured butter over them during the resting period, then serve.

Doreen and Steve Sanderson
Affpuddle

Savoury Rice

INGREDIENTS	imperial	metric
Long grain rice, white or brown	4 oz	110 g
Oil	1 tbs	15 ml
Onion, finely chopped	1	1
Cooked meat, chopped into small pieces	4 oz	110 g
Stock cube, chicken or beef	1	1
Water, boiling	½ pint	290 ml
Carrots, chopped or grated	2	2
Red pepper, chopped	½	½
Peas, frozen	2 oz	60 g
Parsley, chopped	+	+
Parmesan	+	+

Heat the oil and add the onion and pepper and fry until soft.

Add the rice and mix well. Dissolve the stock cube in the boiling water and add to the rice. Bring to boil and reduce to a simmer. Add the remaining ingredients and cook gently until rice is cooked and water absorbed.

Stir in the Parmesan and parsley.

Serves 2

Kath Wharton
Briantspuddle

Bolognese for Lasagne or Cannelloni

INGREDIENTS	imperial	metric
Lamb or Beef mince	1 lb	500 g
Tomatoes, chopped	14 oz	400 g
Passata	14 oz	400 g
Onion, medium, finely chopped	1	1
Mushrooms, finely chopped	5 oz	150 g
Carrot, grated, (optional, good for getting into children)	1	1
Garlic cloves	2	2
Dried mixed herbs, (or fresh basil and thyme to taste)	2 tsp	10 g
Worcestershire sauce, optional	+	+
Red wine, optional	½ glass	½ glass
Pesto, optional	+	+
Oil and butter	+	+
Lasagne, Cannelloni or Spaghetti	+	+
Cheese, grated, or Parmesan	+	+
Roux sauce, including cheese	1 pint	570 ml

Heat a little olive oil in a frying pan and brown off the meat of your choice. Put the meat in a dish to keep warm and in the same pan, add a little butter and oil and sauté the onions, garlic, mushrooms and carrots until soft. Add the herbs and season to taste.

Add in the chopped tomatoes, passata and optional extras of red wine, pesto and Worcestershire Sauce as desired. Return the meat to the sauce.
Bring to a boil and simmer gently for 30 minutes.

...for Lasagne

Layer bolognese, roux and lasagne sheets, and repeat. Dish approx. **12" x 8"** ¦ **30cm x 20cm**

Top with grated cheese or Parmesan.

Cook at **320°F** ¦ **160°C** ¦ **Gas 3** until golden brown on top.

... for Cannelloni

Allow the sauce to cool a little. Hold the pasta tube over the serving dish, teaspoon mix into cannelloni tubes and lay them down across the dish.

Pour over about ½ **pint** ¦ **300ml** roux.

Top with grated cheese.

Cook at **320°F** ¦ **160°C** ¦ **Gas 3** until golden brown on top.

...for a low fat, low salt version that's also suitable for babies and small children

Optional - substitute the beef or lamb mince for diced chicken or Quorn™

Lightly fry the mince using fat from mince, drain off any excess oil and rinse with boiling water to drain off fat.

To avoid frying the vegetables in oil, sweat the onions in the microwave for 5 minutes, stirring them mid-way through cooking. Cook the mushrooms and then the carrots in the same way. Mix the vegetables and the meat together along with herbs and stir in the chopped tomatoes and passata. Cook gently for about 30 minutes.

If cooking for small children to serve with spaghetti, cook the sauce a little further. The sauce can be blended for babies.

This freezes well.

Kerrie Hudson-Gorringe
Affpuddle

Green Goddess Chicken

INGREDIENTS	imperial	metric
Chicken	=	=
Mayonnaise	=	=
Crème fraîche, or sour cream	=	=
Tarragon, finely chopped	+	+
White wine vinegar	½ tbs	10 ml
Spring onions, finely chopped	1 tbs	20 g

Mix equal portions of mayonnaise, crème fraîche (or sour cream). The volume depends on the amount of cooked chicken you have.

Add finely chopped tarragon to taste.

Add the white wine vinegar (or cider vinegar or tarragon vinegar).

Add a tablespoon of finely chopped spring onion.

Mix well.

Add to your cooked diced chicken.

Serve with new potatoes or rice.

Brilliant for posh picnics and cold lunches – a no cook sauce with easy serving !

Lesley Haskins
Briantspuddle

Mexican Winter Warmer

INGREDIENTS	imperial	metric
Tortillas	8	8
Peppers, all colours, chopped	1½	1½
Onion, medium, finely chopped	1	1
Mushrooms	5 oz	150 g
Chicken or Mixed Beans, (400g tin)	1lb	500 g
Crème fraîche	1 pint	570 ml
Paprika	1 tsp	5 ml
Cayenne	1 tsp	5 ml
Coriander	1 tsp	5 ml
Turmeric, optional	1 tsp	5 ml
Cumin	1 tsp	5 ml
Chilli powder	1 tsp	5 ml
Salsa, a jar of	10 oz	300 g
Salt & Pepper	+	+

Cook chicken and cut into bite sized pieces.
Cook the onions and peppers until soft.
Cook the mushrooms until soft and add to the onions and peppers.
On a low heat add all the seasoning and thoroughly mix. Add the salsa and fold in chicken or mixed beans for a vegetarian option.

Lay a generous spoonful of mix at one end of the tortilla, roll up and lay seam down into the baking dish. If any mix remains pour over the top.
Pour the crème fraîche over the top and scatter with grated cheddar or mozzarella

Oven **320°F | 160°C | Gas 3** 20-30 mins until golden brown and bubbling.

Serve with green salad and potato wedges.

Kerrie Hudson-Gorringe
Affpuddle

Bean Lasagne

INGREDIENTS	imperial	metric
Cooked mixed beans	½ lb	230 g
Mushrooms, sliced	¼ lb	110 g
Chilli powder	1 tsp	5 ml
Red wine	1 glass	1 glass
Yoghurt	5 oz	140 g
Onion, chopped	1	1
Pepper, chopped	1	1
Ground cumin	1 tsp	5 ml
Cream cheese	5 oz	140 g
Lasagne sheets, pre-cooked	6	6
Garlic clove	1	1
Tomatoes, chopped	14 oz	400 g
Cheese, grated	3 oz	90 g
Salt & Pepper	+	+

Sauté the onion, mushroom, pepper and garlic in olive oil. Add the beans, tomatoes, spices, seasoning and wine. Simmer on a low heat for 1½ hours.

Mix the cream cheese and yoghurt. Lightly grease a baking dish and put a layer of bean mix, then lasagne sheets and a layer of the cream cheese/yoghurt mix. Repeat, ending with cream cheese/yoghurt mix.

Top with the grated cheese and slices of tomato and mushroom dotted with oil.

Bake at **350°F ¦ 175°C ¦ Gas 4** for 20 minutes or until golden.

Taken from the 'Down to Earth' recipe collection and served by the Briantspuddle Village Hall Committee at many a harvest lunch in the 1980's and '90's

Mary Nesling
Briantspuddle

Spinach, Chicken and Bacon

INGREDIENTS	imperial	metric
Chicken breast	10 oz	300 g
Bacon, unsmoked back	6 slices	6 slices
Spinach	+	+
Olive oil	+	+
Parmesan cheese, shavings	+	+
Pesto or Italian dressing	+	+

Remove the stems from the spinach and place the leaves in a large bowl.

Heat the olive oil in a pan and sear the chicken on a high heat until brown, reduce heat and ensure thoroughly cooked. Remove and keep warm.

Fry the bacon in the pan. Remove and cut in to small pieces.

Mix the bacon, chicken and Parmesan shavings (vary to taste) evenly into the spinach.

Mix in the dressing and serve immediately to ensure the meat is hot/warm.

Another dish that Nick creates is one fashioned after we visited an Italian restaurant in Norwich about 15 years ago. It takes as long to make as the meat to cook so is very quick. Unfortunately he doesn't weigh anything!
Here are estimated quantities for four.

Rebecca and Nick Gore
Affpuddle

Pork Crumble

INGREDIENTS	imperial	metric
FILLING		
Pork, diced	1 lb	460 g
Butter	2 oz	60 g
Leeks, sliced	1 lb	460 g
Onion, small, finely chopped	1	1
Carrot, sliced	1	1
Flour	2 oz	60 g
Cider	4 tbs	60 ml
Stock	1 pint	570 ml
Salt & Pepper	+	+
CRUMBLE TOPPING		
Flour	2 oz	60 g
Breadcrumbs, brown	2 oz	60 g
Butter	2 oz	60 g
Grated cheese	2 oz	60 g
Salt & Pepper	+	+

Melt butter and add onions, leeks, carrots and cook until tender. Add pork and lightly brown. Drain and put in an ovenproof dish.

Add flour to remaining fat and cook for 1 minute. Stir in cider and stock and season. Pour over pork.

Cover and cook for approx 45 mins at
350°F ¦ 170°C ¦ Gas 4
Mix crumb mixture and put on top of meat and cook uncovered for a further 30 mins.

A family favourite passed down by Mrs Cutler senior

Karen Cutler
Briantspuddle

Alabama Chilli

INGREDIENTS	imperial	metric
Oil	1 tbs	15 ml
Minced beef	1 lb	460 g
Onions, diced	2	2
Carrot, peeled and diced	1	1
Chilli, diced	1	1
Tomatoes, chopped	14 oz	400 g
Tomato purée	3 tbs	45 ml
Stock	¼ pint	140 ml
Bay leaf	1	1
Chilli powder	½ tsp	3 ml
Mixed herbs	½ tsp	3 ml
Black pepper, freshly ground	+	+
Salt	+	+
Sweetcorn, frozen	8 oz	230 g
Kidney beans, drained	14 oz	400 g

Pre-heat oven to **350°F | 175°C | Gas 4**
Heat the oil in a frying pan and brown off the meat.
Transfer it to a casserole dish.
Sauté the onion, carrot, pepper and chilli and add
to the meat.
Add the remaining ingredients except the
sweetcorn and kidney beans. Season well.

Cook in the oven for 1 hour. Taste and adjust
seasoning as necessary. Remove the bay leaf and
add the sweetcorn and kidney beans and cook for
another half hour.
Serve with rice or on top of a jacket potato with a
green side salad.

Maggie Hoyle
Briantspuddle

Pesto Chicken

INGREDIENTS	imperial	metric
Chicken breasts, skinless	2	2
Parma ham	2-3 slices	2-3 slices
Pesto	1 tbs	15 ml
Black olives, pitted	1 oz	30 g

Oven: **400°F | 200°C | Gas 6**

Chop the olives and mix with the pesto.
Place the chicken breasts between two pieces of cling film. Using a rolling pin flatten out the chicken.
Remove the cling film. Divide the pesto mix between the two chicken breasts and spread on to the meat. Roll up the chicken and then wrap each roll in Parma ham.

Secure the rolled chicken and ham with cooks' string or cocktail sticks.

Place on a baking tray and cook for 20-25 minutes.

Serve with sweet potatoes, roasted tomatoes and broccoli.

Chris Ralls
Briantspuddle

Faggots

INGREDIENTS	imperial	metric
Liver	½ lb	230 g
Pork belly	½ lb	230 g
Onions	6 oz	170 g
Fresh breadcrumbs or Oatmeal	10 oz	290 g
Shredded suet	3 oz	90 g
Garlic, finely minced	+	+
Sage, chopped	½ tsp	3 ml
Flour	1 tbs	15 ml
Beef stock	1 pint	570 ml
Parsley, chopped	+	+
Salt & Pepper	+	+

Large sheet of foil, buttered.

Pre-heat oven to **350°F ¦ 170°C ¦ Gas 4**

Finely mince the meats, onion and garlic.
Add the suet and breadcrumbs/oats, sage and
season with salt and pepper. Combine all the
ingredients together well.
Dust your hands and work surface with flour and
form the mixture into balls.
Lay the foil onto a baking sheet and lay the faggots
onto one half of the buttered foil. Fold the other
half of the sheet over to form a pocket.

Bake in the oven for about 30 minutes.
Remove faggots from the foil and place into a large
pan.
Dissolve the flour in a spoonful of cold water
and add to the stock. Pour the stock around the
faggots.
Heat gently until the stock thickens and carefully
turn the faggots.

Garnish with the parsley

Mike Rabjohns
Briantspuddle

Pheasant Casserole

INGREDIENTS	imperial	metric
Pheasant	1	1
Port wine	1 pint	570 ml
Redcurrant jelly	½ lb	230 g
Orange, rind and juice	1	1
Butter	2 oz	60 g
Flour	+	+
Stock	¼ pint	140 ml
Salt & Pepper	+	+

Cut the pheasant into quarters and roll in the flour seasoned with salt and pepper.

Melt the butter and brown the pieces of pheasant, taking care not to crowd the pan with meat.

Transfer the browned meat to a casserole dish and add the port wine and stock.

Simmer gently for ¾ hour or put on top of the Aga for ¾ hour.

Add the grated zest of one orange and the juice, the redcurrant jelly and continue to simmer until the meat is tender and just falling off the bone (approx. 1 hour).

Sarah Lowman
Briantspuddle

Fruited Venison in Burgundy

INGREDIENTS	imperial	metric
Butter	1 oz	30 g
Olive oil	1 tbs	15 ml
Garlic cloves, crushed	2	2
Onion, chopped	8 oz	230 g
Casserole Venison, cubed	1½ lb	700 g
Worcestershire sauce	1 tbs	15 ml
Red wine, Burgundy or a rich, fruity red	½ pint	290 ml
Apricots, dried, ready to eat	3 oz	90 g
Orange, rind and juice	1	1
Tomato purée	2 tbs	30 ml
Celery stalks, chopped	2	2
Carrots, chopped	6 oz	170 g
Parsnips, chopped	4 oz	110 g
Bouquet garni	1	1
Salt	2 tsp	10 ml
Sugar, light brown	2 tbs	30 ml
Flour	2 tbs	30 ml
Water	3 tbs	45 ml

Melt butter and oil and brown the meat. Add the onions and garlic and fry until soft. Add all the remaining ingredients apart from flour and water. Mix well and bring to a boil, stirring well.

Cover the casserole with a lid and place in the oven. **325°F ¦ 160°C ¦ Gas 3**
Cook for 2½-3 hours until meat is tender.

Remove from the oven and stand over a low heat on the hob.

Mix flour and water smoothly and add to the venison mixture.

Remove the bouquet garni and simmer for 5 minutes before serving.

Diana Holman
Affpuddle

Something sweet

Bramble Mousse

INGREDIENTS	imperial	metric
Blackberries, washed	1 lb	500 g
Gelatine, leaf	¼ oz	7 g
Lemon, juiced	½	½
Eggs, large	3	3
Caster sugar	4 oz	110 g
Double cream	7 fl oz	200 ml

Keep about **2oz ¦ 50g** of the nicest looking blackberries for serving.

Put the rest into a saucepan, cover and cook gently for 5 minutes until softened. Soak the gelatine leaves in a shallow dish of cold water to soften.

Crush the cooked blackberries in the saucepan using a potato masher, then sieve into a bowl, pressing with the back of a wooden spoon to extract as much juice as possible.

Rinse the saucepan and add the blackberry juice into the pan, along with the lemon juice and heat gently until almost simmering, then take off the heat.

Squeeze the gelatine leaves to remove excess water, then add them to the hot blackberry juice and stir until dissolved. Set aside to cool.

In a bowl, whisk the eggs with the caster sugar until thick and pale. Whilst continuing to whisk, slowly pour in the blackberry juice, followed by **¼ pint ¦ 150ml** of the cream.

Pour the mixture into a serving dish or glasses and refrigerate for a couple of hours until set.

Before serving decorate with the remaining blackberries and some cream.

Sarah Lowman
Briantspuddle

Baked Bananas

INGREDIENTS	imperial	metric
Bananas, 1 large one per person		
Butter		
Brown sugar		
Sultanas		
Hazelnuts		
Sherry		
Cream		

A good way to use up ripe bananas.

Peel them and lay them out in a flat dish.

Dot with generous helpings of butter, brown sugar,
sultanas, hazel nuts, and slosh with some sherry
and cream.

Bake until they look soft and golden brown.

Frances Solly
Affpuddle

Baked Apples

INGREDIENTS	imperial	metric
Apples, 1 large one per person		
Butter		
Brown sugar		
Sultanas		
Hazelnuts		
Sherry		
Cream		

The same ingredients as 'Baked Bananas' (p.132) serve for apples.

Choose a big apple for each person, core them first, and then stuff their cores with sultanas, nuts, brown sugar, butter. Slit the skin round the widest part.

Butter, cream and sherry can be added to taste.

Bake in a hot oven until the apples are nearly bursting out of their skins.

Serve with ice-cream, crumble, custard or cream.

Frances Solly
Affpuddle

134

B.B.C. Pudding

INGREDIENTS	imperial	metric
Flour	8 lb	3.6 kg
Breadcrumbs	8 lb	3.6 kg
Suet	4 lb	1.8 kg
Sugar	1 lb	460 g
Salt	2 oz	60 g
Marmalade	3 lb 2 oz	1.4 kg
Cherries	½ lb	230 g
if Suet is unavailable use: Dripping	4 lb	1.8 kg
Baking powder	4 oz	110 g

RAF Manual of Cooking and Dietary

With all suet puddings, flour or flour and breadcrumbs form our foundation. Breadcrumbs should be used wherever possible as they assist in making puddings lighter and it is a good way of utilising old bread. If suet is unavailable, use dripping and baking powder.

Sieve the flour and salt into a clean trough then add the sugar, breadcrumbs, shredded suet and thoroughly mix. If using dripping, work the fat into the flour before adding breadcrumbs. Use the marmalade together with water for mixing purposes.

Cut the cherries into halves and arrange in microphone shape at the bottom of each greased pudding basin and cover with the suet mixture.

Cover with greased proof or pudding cloths and steam for approximately 3 hours.

The recipe fascinates me because of the story behind it.

When my mother passed away, I found a book amongst her possessions which she was given on joining the R.A.F. during the war as a cook. One of the recipes in the book is called B.B.C. PUDDING. A suet pudding with marmalade and cherries.

I was intrigued at the name but realised after reading the method why it was so called. It was the positioning of the cherries in the bowls.

*The quantities of ingredients appear substantial however all the recipes in the book are based on requirements **per hundred men**.*

(Not sure what happened about feeding the women!).

Mel Parks
Briantspuddle

see overleaf

A.P. 87,
Revised Edition.
April, 1942.

R.A.F. MANUAL OF COOKING AND DIETARY

Promulgated for the information and guidance of all concerned.

By Command of the Air Council,

AIR MINISTRY.

Method.—Add the currants, peel, nutmeg, spice and the rind
...ce of the lemons to the foundation. The lemon juice is usually
...led with the water whilst mixing.

215.

Raisin Pudding
5 lbs. Raisins.

Method.—Add the raisins to the dry ingredients and mix down with

...6.
12 ozs. Cocoa.

Alice Pudding
8 ozs. Egg Powder.   2 lbs. Jam.

...od.—Divide the foundation into three separate portions. Add
...one, jam to the second and egg powder to the third. Place in
...oportions into the greased pudding basins.

Currant Pudding
4 lbs. Currants.
1 lb. Peel.

—Add the currants and peel to the foundation and mix
...water.

...urrants.
Schoolboy Pudding
1 oz. Spice.   2 lbs. Apple Rings.

Soak the apple rings, chop and add to the foundation
...currants and spice. Mix down with water.

...rants.
...ns.
Windsor Pudding
1 lb. Peel.
2 lbs. Potatoes.   2 lbs. Carrots.

...the currants, raisins and peel to the foundation.
...rots and potatoes, sprinkle a few grated carrots into
...ch greased pudding basin and add the rest into the
...down with water.

Ginger Pudding
3½ lbs. Treacle.
8 ozs. Ginger.

...e ginger to the foundation and use treacle and
...poses.

Plum Pudding
2 lbs. Treacle.
3 Lemons.
1 oz. of Nutmeg and Spice.

...be used instead of Breadcrumbs.

58

Method.—Add the currants, raisins, peel, nutmeg, spice and rind
and juice of the lemons to the foundation. Use the treacle and water
for mixing purposes.

No. 222.
Plain Suet Pudding
12 lbs. Flour.
2 ozs. Salt.   3 lbs. Suet.

Method.—Sift the flour and salt together, add shredded suet and
mix thoroughly. Mix down with water and place into greased pudding
basins.

No. 223.
B.B.C. Pudding
3½ lbs. Marmalade.
½ lb. Cherries.

Method.—Cut the cherries into halves and arrange in microphone
shape at the bottom of each greased pudding basin. Use the marmalade together with water for mixing purposes.

No. 224.
Marina Pudding
2 lbs. Desiccated Coconut.
1½ lbs. Cocoa.

Method.—Place a little desiccated coconut into the bottom of each
greased pudding basin. Add the rest of the coconut to the foundation,
mix the cocoa to a paste with water and use the paste for mixing
purposes.

No. 225.
Hobart Pudding
4 lbs. Raisins.
8 ozs. Egg Powder.   2 lbs. Apple Rings.

Method.—Soak the apple rings, chop and add to the foundation
together with raisins and egg powder. Mix down with water.

No. 226.
Cabinet Pudding
4 lbs. Sultanas.
8 ozs. Egg Powder.

Method.—Add the sultanas to the foundation. Dilute the egg
powder with water and use the liquid for mixing purposes.

No. 227.
Apple and Date Pudding
6 lbs. Fresh Apples (Sliced).   4 lbs. Dates (Chopped).
2 Lemons.

Method.—Arrange two or three slices of apple at the bottom of each
greased pudding basin. Add the remaining apples, dates and grated
lemon rind to the foundation. Use water containing the lemon juice
for mixing purposes.

No. 228.
Army Crusader Pudding
2 lbs. Sultanas.   1 lb. Carrots.
2 lbs. Raisins.   3 lbs. Jam.

59

Hot Cross Buns and Apricot Butter Pudding

INGREDIENTS	imperial	metric
Hot Cross buns	4	4
Butter	2 oz	60 g
Eggs, beaten	3	3
Greek yoghurt	7 oz	200 g
Apricots, dried, chopped	4½ oz	125 g
Soft brown sugar	2 oz	60 g
Milk	10 fl oz	290 ml

Preheat oven to **350°F ¦ 180°C ¦ Gas 4**

Slice buns vertically into thick slices and butter on one side of each slice.

Grease an ovenproof dish with butter and arrange the bun slices on the base slightly overlapping.

Scatter chopped apricots over the slices.

Place beaten eggs, milk, yoghurt and sugar in a bowl and whisk thoroughly. Pour the mixture over the buns.

Place the dish in a large roasting tin and fill the tin with boiling water until it comes halfway up the side of the dish.

Bake for 30-40 minutes until the custard is set.

Serve with cream or yoghurt.

This recipe comes from my Aunty Lorna who is ninety four.

Irene Bryant
Briantspuddle

Key Lime Pie

INGREDIENTS	imperial	metric
Short crust pastry	9 oz	250 g
Eggs, large	3	3
Condensed milk, tinned	14 fl oz	400 ml
Lime juice, (approx. 5-6 limes)	4½ fl oz	125 ml
Cream of tartare	¼ tsp	2 ml
Caster sugar	2 oz	50 g
Limes, finely grated zest	2	2

Heat the oven to **400°F | 200°C | Gas 6**
Line a **10" | 23cm** flan tin with shortcrust pastry and bake blind for 12 minutes, then remove the paper and beans and bake for a further 6-8 minutes.

Separate the eggs. Beat the yolks until thick, add the condensed milk, and slowly beat in the lime juice. Continue beating until the mixture thickens. Pour into the pastry case.

Whisk the egg whites until they are frothy, add the cream of tartare then, gradually, the caster sugar. Continue whisking until the meringue stands up in stiff peaks, then pile the mixture on top of the filling, and sprinkle over the lime zest.

Return to the oven for 8-10 minutes for the meringue to set. Leave to cool so that the filling can set before cutting.

I found this recipe about thirty years ago and I've made it hundreds of times! I enjoy making this pie and love its zesty lime taste combined with the softness of the meringue.

Mel Parks
Briantspuddle

Lemon Cheesecake

INGREDIENTS	imperial	metric
BASE		
Digestive biscuits	6 oz	170 g
Butter, melted	1 oz	30 g
FILLING		
Soft cheese, full fat	14 oz	400 g
Lemon, large, zested	1	1
Lemon juice	4 tbs	60 ml
Caster sugar	4 oz	110 g
Crème fraîche	4 tbs	60 ml
Egg	1	1
Icing sugar, optional – for dusting	+	+

Pre-heat the oven to **320°F** ¦ **160°C** ¦ **Gas 3**
Line the base of an **7"** ¦ **18cm** round spring form
tin with non-stick baking parchment.

Base
To make the base, put the digestive biscuits and
butter in a food processor and mix until evenly
broken in to a coarse crumb mix. Alternatively
place the ingredients in a plastic bag and bash with
a rolling pin. Press the mix into the tin to make an
even base. Bake the base for 10 minutes.

Aga method.

*Two door Aga – bake on the grid shelf on the floor
of the Roasting Oven with the cold plain shelf set
on the runners above for 15 minutes until it begins
to colour.*

Filling
Place all the ingredients for the filling in a food
processor and blend until smooth. Spoon the
mixture on to the biscuit base and spread evenly.

Bake for 20 minutes until just set.

Two door Aga – bake on the grid shelf on the floor of the Roasting Oven with the cold plain shelf just above for 25 minutes.

Transfer the plain shelf to middle of the simmering oven. Position the cheesecake tin on this shelf towards the back for a further 15 minutes.

Four door Aga – with the grid shelf on the fourth set of runners in the Baking Oven, cook the cheesecake for 40-45 minutes until just set.

Leave the cheesecake to cool in the tin. Loosen the edges with a palette knife and open the spring lock to release. Serve warm or cold and dusted with icing sugar.

Mary Nesling
Briantspuddle

149

Mississippi Mud Pie

INGREDIENTS	imperial	metric
BASE		
Ginger nut biscuits, crushed	3 oz	90 g
Digestive biscuits, crushed	3 oz	90 g
Butter, melted	2 oz	60 g
FILLING		
Marshmallows	12 oz	340 g
Milk	1 tbs	15 ml
Double cream	17 fl oz	490 ml
Rum	4 tbs	60 ml
Coffee, cold	4 tsp	20 ml
70% Dark chocolate	12 oz	340 g

Base

Mix the crushed biscuits with melted butter. Place into base of a spring form tin or into a flan dish lined with non-stick paper.

Filling

Melt marshmallows with milk, stirring to mix well. Allow to cool. Whip the cream. Mix rum and coffee into marshmallow mixture. Melt chocolate and blend into mixture together with whipped cream. Pour on to the biscuit base and refrigerate for three hours.

A 1970's recipe that I think is well worth reviving as it is so gloriously, shamelessly rich and alcoholic!

Diana Holman
Affpuddle

Rhubarb Flummery

INGREDIENTS	imperial	metric
Rhubarb	1 lb	460 g
Sugar	6 oz	170 g
Water	½ pint	290 ml
Flour	1 tbs	15 ml
Gelatine, powder	2 tsp	10 ml
Orange, grated rind	1	1
Orange liqueur	1 tbs	15 ml

Wash the rhubarb and cut into **1"** ¦ **2.5cm** lengths.

Make a sugar syrup with the sugar and water, and cook the rhubarb until tender. Drain. Thicken with the flour blended with **1 tbs** ¦ **15ml** of cold syrup. Add the powdered gelatine softened in **2 tbs** ¦ **30ml** of cold water.

Add the grated rind of an orange and when it is quite cold whisk until it thickens and fold in the stewed rhubarb and orange liqueur.

Serve in glasses covered with clotted cream.

We lived at No 33 Briantspuddle for 41 years and David grew superb rhubarb, which we inherited from the Stockley family. Hence this favourite recipe.

Tasie Russell
Briantspuddle

'Stink Puff'

INGREDIENTS	imperial	metric
SAUCE		
Strawberries, tinned	8 oz	230 g
Caster sugar	3 oz	90 g
Lemon, juiced	½	½
FOOL MIX		
Strawberry jelly	5 oz	140 g
Carnation™ milk, small tin	6 oz	170 g

*I'll give the recipe as I received it, but actually I normally replace the tinned strawberries (which was probably all that was available most of the year in the 1960's) with ½ **pint ¦ 290ml** of strawberry sauce which is how I have always frozen surplus strawberries. If you make the pudding using semi-thawed sauce it sets very quickly and is less likely to separate. The colour is also much better using sauce rather than tinned fruit.*

Sauce

Blend strawberries, caster sugar and lemon together and pass through a sieve. Add jelly melted in ¼ **pint ¦ 140ml** of hot water.

Fool Mix

Whisk Carnation™ milk until very stiff and add to sauce mixture. Leave until cold.

This is a kind of strawberry fool my mother used to make which never had a name and was just called Pink Stuff. My father was given to making spoonerisms so it became Stink Puff, which it is to this day and to the grandchildren's delight.

Lindy Ventham
Briantspuddle

Lemon Meringue Pie

INGREDIENTS	imperial	metric
PASTRY		
Flour	8 oz	230 g
Salt	½ tsp	3 ml
Butter, unsalted	6 oz	170 g
Sugar	2 tbs	30 ml
Lemon juice	3 tbs	45 ml
Water	3 tbs	45 ml
Lemon, grated rind	+	+
CRUMB LAYER		
Sugar	2 tbs	30 ml
Breadcrumbs, white	2 tbs	30 ml
Cardamom seeds, ground	½ tsp	3 ml
LEMON LAYER		
Sugar	7 oz	200 g
Eggs, well beaten	3	3
Butter, unsalted	8 oz	230 g
Lemons, rind and strained juice	2	2
MERINGUE		
Eggs, whites	6	6
Caster sugar	7 oz	200 g
Sugar	+	+

Make pastry in the usual way with the first six ingredients. Chill for 30 minutes, then roll out and line a **10" ¦ 25cm** tart tin with removable base. Prick the base, brush with melted butter and bake at **375°F ¦ 190°C ¦ Gas 5** for 30 minutes. Mix sugar, crumbs and cardamom seeds and put immediately into the pastry when it comes from the oven.

Have the lemon curd ready – beat the first three ingredients in a pan. Stir over a low heat, adding the butter in bits. When the mixture is hot, (keep it well below boiling point) pour it over the crumb-lined pastry. Return to the oven for 10 minutes, until the filling is just set, but still a little shaky in the middle. Leave to cool.

Beat the egg whites until stiff, add the caster sugar gradually, beating again after each addition.

Pipe or pile on to the tart; take it right to the pastry rim so that the lemon filling is covered entirely.

Put the pie into the oven again at **375°F ¦ 190°C ¦ Gas 5** for 10-15 minutes, until the meringue is browned.

This is a recipe I came across 30 years ago for the first time. It is a sure fire success and has a mystery ingredient that never fails to intrigue guests. It's a big pudding so it fits any occasion. You will find you need enough for second helpings, it's that popular.

I also like this pudding because it comes from an era when no photos accompanied the recipe. This means I'm reassured that I have been able to recreate the splendour of the original every time!

Sue Jones
Turnerspuddle

Syllabub

INGREDIENTS	imperial	metric
Caster sugar	6 oz	170 g
Lemons, juiced and grated rinds	2	2
Sherry	2 fl oz	60 ml
Brandy	2 fl oz	60 ml
Double cream	1 pint	570 ml

Soak the lemon rind in the lemon juice for at least 3 hours.

After the soaking time, strain the lemon juice over the sugar.

Stir in the sherry and brandy and pour in the cream.

Beat the mixture until it becomes fluffy, but don't over beat otherwise it will turn to butter.

Pile the mixture in individual glasses or bowls.

Chill for at least 12 hours.

Mary Nesling
Briantspuddle

Treacle Tart with Ginger

INGREDIENTS	imperial	metric
PASTRY		
Sweet shortcrust pastry	14 oz	400 g
FILLING		
Golden syrup	1 lb 10 oz	750 g
Breadcrumbs or Oatmeal	8 oz	230 g
Ground ginger	1½ tsp	10 ml
Stem ginger, very finely chopped	+	+
Lemon, juice and zest	1	1
Eggs	3	3

Use a **10"** ¦ **23cm** tart case, about **1"** ¦ **3cm** deep. Roll out the pastry, line the tart case and chill for 30 minutes.

Oven **400°F** ¦ **200°C** ¦ **Gas 6**
Line the pastry with baking parchment and baking beans and bake blind for 20 mins. Remove the beans and paper, bake for another 10 mins until pale gold.

Reduce oven temp to **285°F** ¦ **140°C** ¦ **Gas 1**

Mix golden syrup, breadcrumbs, lemon zest, ginger, eggs together and pour into the pastry case. Bake for about 55 minutes until golden & suntanned and it feels set to the fingertips.

Let some vanilla ice cream sit out of the freezer until very easily scooped. Mix together one scoop of ice cream to one scoop of clotted cream and dollop on top of the warm tart. Drizzle over a little of the juice from the stem ginger jar.

A favourite of my Father's. As I child, I remember watching him make it and annoying him with my new found, but limited cooking knowledge, telling him he should be rubbing the flour and butter with his fingertips rather than man-handling it.
Of course his pastry was melt in the mouth !

Leonora Sheppard
Briantspuddle

Oma's White Pudding

INGREDIENTS	imperial	metric
Plain yoghurt, low fat	17 oz	500 g
Elmlea™ double cream alternative	½ pint	284 ml
Vanilla sugar	+	+

Whip the Elmlea™ until it is really stiff and add the vanilla sugar.

Fold in the yoghurt and mix together.   Voila!

This makes a really smooth creamy pudding which you can serve with red fruit and biscuits.

When I was a child visiting my grandparents in Holland in the early 1960's, the milk was still delivered fresh from the farm. Every morning the milk cart would come down the street (which had sandy side pavements and a road made of small red bricks laid in a herringbone pattern). The milkman would ring a bell, and all the housewives would come out with their milk pans to collect the unpasteurised milk which was then taken home and boiled on the stove.

My grandmother stored the boiled milk in the cellar. We had to drink a glass of milk every morning. It often had bits of skin in it which made me shudder. I used to drink it while holding my nose to stop the smell of boiled milk from making me gag.

If we were really lucky we were given buttermilk to drink and we were allowed to put a teaspoon of soft brown sugar in it. The Dutch are great dairy farmers and before yoghurt appeared in England we would have great bowls of it as a child. This recipe is one I inherited from my mother and which my children called "Oma's white pudding". It's very simple.

I make my own vanilla sugar by adding vanilla pods to icing sugar and storing it in a glass jar. You could of course use full fat yoghurt and double cream if your conscience and diet allows ....

Kate Gainsford
Briantspuddle

Warming Winter Fruit Tart

INGREDIENTS	imperial	metric
Pineapple, sliced in two, top to bottom	1	1
Satsumas, peeled and sectioned into small pieces	6	6
Butter	2 oz	60 g
Demerara sugar	3 tbs	45 ml
Dark rum	2 fl oz	60 ml
Stem ginger, cut into small pieces	2	2

Scoop out the flesh from the pineapple and discard the core. Keep the two shells of the pineapple skin. Cut up the fruit into small pieces.

Heat up the butter in a large frying pan and add all the fruit.

Stir until the fruit is covered in the hot butter and looks tender but not brown. Then pour in the rum and scatter sugar over it. When it's all hot, pour into the pineapple skin shells.

Optional – pour over a little warmed brandy or rum and light with a match – Whoosh !

Serve with cream or plain yoghurt.

Audrey Grindrod
Briantspuddle

Aunt Cynthia's Chocolate Sauce

INGREDIENTS	imperial	metric
Golden syrup	2 tbs	30 ml
Cocoa powder	2 tbs	30 ml
Water	2 tbs	30 ml

Gently heat and stir all together

Lindy Ventham
Briantspuddle

Caramel Apple Cake

INGREDIENTS	imperial	metric
Butter, softened	4½ oz	125 g
Carnation Caramel™	14 oz	397 g
Eggs, medium	2	2
Self-raising flour, sifted	8 oz	230 g
Baking powder	2 tsp	10 ml
Ground cinnamon, or mixed spice	2 tsp	10 ml
Bramley apples, peeled, cored and diced	10 oz	300 g
Milk, semi-skimmed	2 tbs	30 ml
Demerara sugar	1 tbs	15 ml

Preheat oven to **300°F ┆ 150°C ┆ Gas 2**

Place the butter with **8oz ┆ 225g** of the caramel in a large bowl and beat with electric whisk until well combined. Then beat in the eggs one at a time.

Sift over the flour, baking powder and spice. Fold together then gently stir in the apple and the milk.

Lightly butter and base line a **8" ┆ 20cm** spring-form cake tin. Spoon in the cake mix, smooth the top and scatter the demerara sugar on the top.

Bake for 1 hour or until risen and lightly golden on top. Remove the cake from the tin and place on a serving plate.

Warm the rest of the caramel in a small saucepan over a low heat until pourable then drizzle over the top of the cake.

Serve with a dollop of ice cream or a dollop of whipped cream or simply with a cup of tea!

Perfect when there's a good crop of Bramley apples.

Shirley Prideaux
Affpuddle

Biscotti

INGREDIENTS	imperial	metric
Nuts, whole, skinned almonds and hazelnuts	7 oz	200 g
Eggs	2	2
Golden caster sugar	6 oz	170 g
Plain flour	10 oz	290 g
Baking powder, sifted with the flour	1 tsp	5 ml
Butter, melted	1½ tbs	25 ml

Preheat oven to **325°F ¦ 170°C ¦ Gas 3**

Put the nuts on a baking sheet and toast for no more than 10 minutes until pale gold and fragrant. Remove from the oven and allow to cool. Turn the temperature down to **300°F ¦ 150°C ¦ Gas 2**

Whisk together the eggs and sugar until glossy and bubbly. Add the flour and baking powder and nuts and work in to a dough.
Dust the worktop with extra flour, shape the dough into a long smooth roll about **2" ¦ 5cm** wide and

1" ¦ 2.5cm high. Push any wayward nuts back into the dough so they do not burn during cooking.

Place the dough on a baking sheet lined with parchment and bake for 20-25 minutes until firm and risen. Place on a rack to cool. When cool, use a good serrated knife to cut **½" ¦ 1cm** slices. Place the slices back on the baking sheet, brush with the melted butter and bake until crisp, approx. 10-12 minutes.

Delicious served warm.

Trish Kilbank
Briantspuddle

Moist Chocolate Cake with Fudge Icing

INGREDIENTS	imperial	metric
CAKE		
Margarine	4 oz	110 g
Caster sugar	4 oz	110 g
Golden syrup	8 oz	230 g
Milk	¼ pint	140 ml
Flour, self-raising	8 oz	230 g
Cocoa	1 oz	30 g
Egg, large	1	1
FUDGE ICING		
Margarine	2 oz	60 g
Milk	3 tbs	45 ml
Icing sugar	8 oz	230 g
Cocoa	1 oz	30 g

Cake

Oven **350°F ¦ 150°C ¦ Gas 2**

Grease and line an **8" ¦ 20cm** cake tin.

Place the margarine, sugar, syrup and milk into a saucepan and heat gently until melted.

Leave to cool.

Sift the cocoa and flour into a mixing bowl.

Add the cooled mixture and the egg.

Beat together until smooth.

Pour into the cake tin.

Bake 1¼ - 1½ hours until the top is shiny and a skewer comes out clean.

Fudge Icing

Place all the ingredients in a saucepan and heat gently until everything is melted.

Leave to cool completely and then beat well.

Spread the fudge topping over the top of the cake.

Chris Ralls
Briantspuddle

Date & Walnut Cake

INGREDIENTS	imperial	metric
Water, boiling	½ pint	290 ml
Dates, chopped	8 oz	230 g
Bicarbonate of soda	1 tsp	5 ml
Sugar	8 oz	230 g
Butter	3 oz	90 g
Egg, beaten	1	1
Plain flour	10 oz	290 g
Walnuts	2 oz	60 g
Baking powder	1 tsp	5 ml
Salt	1 tsp	5 ml

Put water, dates and bicarbonate of soda in a bowl together. Leave to stand for 5 minutes.

Cream sugar and butter together, stir in the egg with the water and dates.

Sieve flour with baking powder and salt. Fold in walnuts. Pour mixture into a greased, lined **8"** ¦ **20cm** tin.

Bake in a moderate oven for 1 hour.

This is a recipe that was given to me many, many years ago by my mother-in-law. She made this cake and a fruit cake every week and they ended up in my father-in-law's lunch box each day for over 30 years. Two slices sealed together by a healthy slice of butter. He enjoyed cake and coffee every morning and lived to the ripe old age of ninety.

Sue Jones
Turnerspuddle

Recipe as above with additional topping :

3 oz	85 g	Brown sugar
2 oz	60 g	Butter
2 tbs	30 ml	Cream from top of milk

Mix the above and boil for 3 minutes.
Spread on cooked cake.
Sprinkle with chopped walnuts.

The story goes that it was the wish of H.M Queen Elizabeth the Queen Mother, Commandant in Chief of Women's Royal Army Corps., that this recipe should be sold for 5 pence for any charity.

Erica Moriarty
Briantspuddle

Chocolate Goo

INGREDIENTS	imperial	metric
Digestive biscuits, crushed	4 oz	110 g
Butter	4 oz	110 g
Sultanas	5 oz	140 g
Golden syrup	½ fl oz	15 ml
Drinking chocolate powder	¼ oz	10 g
Bar of chocolate, large, milk or dark	1	1

Gently melt the butter and syrup in a pan over a low heat.

Add the drinking chocolate, sultanas and crushed biscuits and combine.

Press the mix into a tin approx **7" x 8" ¦ 18 x 20cm** and cover with the melted chocolate.

Place in the fridge to set and go firm.

A family favourite given to me by an old friend.

Maggie Hoyle
Briantspuddle

Mrs Martin's Ginger Cake

INGREDIENTS	imperial	metric
Self-raising flour	10 oz	290 g
Butter	6 oz	170 g
Demerara sugar	8 oz	230 g
Eggs	2	2
Salt	1 tsp	5 ml
Powdered ginger	2 tsp	10 ml
Nutmeg, grated	½ tsp	3 ml
Raisins, optional	3 oz	90 g
Walnuts, chopped, optional	2 oz	60 g
Golden syrup	8 oz	230 g
Milk	¼ pint	140 ml

Grease and line two loaf tins approx.
7½" x 9½" ¦ 18cm x 23cm

Sieve together flour, salt and spices. Melt the butter
with sugar and golden syrup, then leave to cool.

When cooled add to the flour mix and stir in beaten
eggs and then the milk. Add the raisins and walnuts
if using.

Bake for approximately 45 minutes at
350°F ¦ 180°C ¦ Gas 4

Mrs Martin - resident of
Briantspuddle's Cruck Cottage in the 1960's

190

Farmhouse Fruit Cake

INGREDIENTS	imperial	metric
Self-raising flour	12 oz	340 g
Salt, just a pinch	+	+
Demerara sugar	6 oz	170 g
Butter	6 oz	170 g
Mixed fruit	10 oz	290 g
Orange or Lemon, grated rind	1	1
Egg, large, beaten	1	1
Cider	¼ pint	140 ml
Marmalade	2 tbs	30 ml

Pre-heat oven to **350°F ¦ 180°C ¦ Gas 4**
7" ¦ 18cm cake tin – round or square, greased and lined.

Sift the flour and salt together. Stir in the sugar and rub in the butter. Mix in the fruit and grated rind.

Make a well in the centre of the dry ingredients and add the beaten egg, cider and marmalade. Fold all the ingredients together.

Pour mixture into the cake tin and level the surface. Bake on a centre shelf in the oven for 1 hour.

Lower the oven temperature to
300°F ¦ 150°C ¦ Gas 2
and bake until the skewer comes out clean.

Leave the cake to cool in the tin before removing.

This freezes well.

Erica Moriarty
Briantspuddle

Pumpkin Cake

INGREDIENTS	imperial	metric
Sugar, granulated	10 oz	300 g
Salt	1 tsp	5 ml
Flour, plain	8 oz	230 g
Bicarbonate of soda	1 tsp	5 ml
Baking powder	¼ tsp	1 ml
Eggs	2	2
Water	4 fl oz	110 ml
Vegetable oil	4 fl oz	110 ml
Pumpkin	9½ oz	270 g
Nutmeg	½ tsp	2 ml
Cinnamon	½ tsp	2 ml
Cloves, ground	½ tsp	2 ml

Beat the eggs and add the sugar.

Add water and beat in the oil.

Sieve dry ingredients.

Mix in dry ingredients next and the pumpkin last.

Cook for 50-60 minutes at **320°F ¦ 160°C ¦ Gas 3**

It can be cooked in a tray bake tin or as a large cake in an **8" ¦ 20cm** tin.

This recipe for a pumpkin cake I was given in about 1968 by the wife of a Canadian Army Officer who was on a course with Jonathan at the Royal Military College of Science, Shrivenham.
It just shows how long I keep good recipes.

Penny Haigh
Briantspuddle

Lemon & Blueberry Friands

INGREDIENTS	imperial	metric
Plain flour	1 oz	30 g
Eggs, whites	3	3
Butter, unsalted	3½ oz	100 g
Icing sugar	4½ oz	125 g
Ground almonds	3 oz	90 g
Lemon, grated rind	1	1
Blueberries	3 oz	90 g
Icing sugar, for dusting	+	+

I use a fan oven at 180°C which I think equates to conventional **400°F ¦ 200°C ¦ Gas 6**

Generously butter six non-stick friand or muffin tins.

Melt the **3½ oz ¦ 100g** of butter and allow to cool. Using a mixing bowl sift in the icing sugar, flour and add the almonds. Mix together using your fingers.

Whisk the egg whites in another bowl until it makes a light and floppy foam.

Make a hole in the middle of the icing sugar and almond mix, pour in the egg whites and add the grated lemon rind then gently stir in the butter to form a soft batter.

Divide the batter among the tins and sprinkle a handful of blueberries over each cake and bake for 15 to 20 minutes until just firm to the touch and golden brown in colour. Cool in the tins and then turn out and cool on a wire rack.

Dust lightly with icing sugar to serve.

This is a favourite of ours with morning coffee, usually when Nick comes in from work on the weekends!
It takes about 40 minutes and will serve six.

Rebecca Gore
Affpuddle

Lemon & Poppy Seed Loaf Cake

INGREDIENTS	imperial	metric
CAKE		
Self-raising flour	5½ oz	150 g
Baking powder	½ tsp	3 ml
Caster sugar	4 oz	110 g
Butter	4 oz	110 g
Eggs, beaten	2	2
Milk, just a little	+	+
Lemon, grated zest	1	1
Poppy seeds	1 tbs	15 ml
ICING		
Caster sugar	2 oz	60 g
Lemon juice	1 tbs	15 ml

Prepare **1lb ¦ 450** loaf tin (ready-made liners work well). Heat oven to **350°F ¦ 180°C ¦ Gas 4**
Cream the butter and sugar until light and fluffy. Gradually add the eggs, a little at a time, beating thoroughly. Gently fold in the sieved flour and baking powder. Add a little milk until the mixture is at dropping consistency. Finally stir in the poppy seeds and lemon zest.
Pile the mixture into the prepared loaf tin and bake for about 30-40 minutes.
Mix the sugar and lemon juice together (it should be runny) and spoon over the loaf while it is still warm.

I travelled to South Africa in 2011 with a Youth Volunteer group and spent the preceding 18 months raising funds and collecting donations. I was generously supported by villagers and visitors to the shop where I worked at weekends. An amazing total of almost £1,350 was raised in the sale of over 400 cakes, baked on Friday evenings after school. Amongst the Dorset Apple Cake, Chocolate Loaf and varied cup cakes was my version of a Lemon and Poppy Seed Loaf Cake which always proved popular!

Josie Griffith
Briantspuddle

Rhubarb Cake

INGREDIENTS	imperial	metric
Self-raising flour	8 oz	230 g
Caster sugar	9½ oz	275 g
Desiccated coconut	4 oz	110 g
Butter, melted	4½ oz	125 g
Eggs, beaten	3	3
Milk	4½ fl oz	125 ml
Vanilla	¼ tsp	2 ml
Rhubarb, finely chopped	3 oz	90 g
Rhubarb stalks	2	2
Demerara sugar	2 tbs	30 ml

Mix together the flour, sugar, coconut and stir in the melted butter, beaten eggs, milk and vanilla.

Put half of this mixture into an **8"** ¦ **20cm** cake tin and scatter on top the chopped rhubarb.

Add the remaining half of the cake mixture and arrange the rhubarb stalks across the top.

Sprinkle the top with demerara sugar.

Bake for 1 hour at **350°F** ¦ **180°C** ¦ **Gas 4**

Serve with a dollop of fresh thick cream.

Store in a cool place as this only keeps for a couple of days.

Toni Hallatt
Briantspuddle

Halloween Cake

INGREDIENTS	imperial	metric
CAKE		
Flour, plain	6 oz	170 g
Baking margarine or butter	3 oz	90 g
Eggs	2	2
Baking powder	1 tsp	5 ml
Sugar	4 oz	110 g
Preserved ginger, chopped	2 oz	60 g
Ginger syrup	1 tbs	15 ml
Milk	3 tbs	45 ml
TOPPING		
Butter	1½ oz	45 g
Soft brown sugar	3 oz	90 g
Almonds, chopped	1 oz	30 g
Glacé cherries and blanched almonds, for decoration	+	+

Grease and line the bottom of an **8" ¦ 20cm** cake tin.

Sift the flour and baking powder together. Cream fat and sugar together until light and fluffy and gradually add the eggs until well mixed.

Stir in the dry ingredients, together with ginger syrup and sufficient milk to a soft consistency.

Lastly stir in the chopped ginger.

Put into the tin, levelling the top, and bake in a moderate oven **320°F ¦ 160°C ¦ Gas 3** for 40 to 45 minutes. Check at 35 minutes.

Make the topping by creaming butter with the sugar, and adding the chopped almonds.

When the cake is cooked, spread the topping mixture on cake, decorate with cherries and blanched almonds.

Place under a hot grill and watch carefully until it's golden brown and bubbling.
   Enjoy.

Next door (No.34), lived two elderly ladies Miss Peters and Miss Clark, the latter was a great baker.

Here is her recipe for a Halloween Cake.

Tasie Russell
Briantspuddle

Vanilla Victoria Sponge

INGREDIENTS	imperial	metric
CAKE		
Self-raising flour	8 oz	230 g
Eggs	4	4
Caster sugar	8 oz	230 g
Baking margarine	8 oz	230 g
Baking powder	1 tsp	5 ml
Vanilla extract	1 tsp	5 ml
FILLING		
Icing sugar	4½ oz	125 g
Butter, unsalted	2 oz	60 g
Vanilla extract	1 tsp	5 ml

Cake

Sift flour and baking powder into a bowl and set to one side. In a mixing bowl, cream together the sugar and margarine until light and fluffy.

Add the beaten eggs and vanilla extract. Gently fold in the flour and baking powder.

Divide the mixture between two lined and greased baking tins **8" ¦ 20cm**

Bake for 20-25 minutes at **320°F ¦ 160°C ¦ Gas 3** until lightly golden and a skewer test comes out clean.

Filling

In a large bowl whisk or beat the butter until light and smooth. Gradually add the icing sugar until fully mixed together and add the vanilla

Spread the filling between the two sponges and dust the top with icing sugar.

For a classic filling, sandwich the cakes together with seedless raspberry jam and enjoy with a cuppa.

Kerrie Hudson-Gorringe
Affpuddle

INDEX

Lightning Source UK Ltd.
Milton Keynes UK
UKOW07n1330040417

298325UK00005B/21/P

9 781527 200548